World Faiths Today Series

Exploring Judais...

Who are your friends? Do you know... them? Do they know everything a...

Well, this is a story about friends who do not know everything about one another. But they are starting to learn some things their friends do and why they do them. Read their story and you might learn something new too!

1 Visiting a synagogue

It was early on Saturday morning and Rees and Sara were sitting in front of the television wearing their coats. The changing pictures and sounds of their favourite TV programme did not interest them today. Their eyes kept wandering to the window. Their ears kept straining for the lightest crunch on the gravel driveway outside. Finally, Sara had had enough.

'I am going to wait outside,' she announced.

Sixteen seconds later both Sara and Rees were swinging on the garden gate. Rees was the first to spot their friends, Dan and Rebecca, walking towards them. Dan and Rebecca were taking them to a Shabbat service at their Reform synagogue. As the friends greeted one another, Sara noticed that Rebecca was wearing a beautiful silver necklace.

'This is the Star of David,' explained Rebecca. 'It is often used to show people that something is Jewish. So, when I wear the Star of David, I am showing people that I am Jewish.'

When they arrived at the synagogue, Sara noticed that the Star of David was there too.

'A synagogue is a place where Jewish people assemble together,' said Dan. 'They gather together for lots of different reasons. Today, Jews are gathering together to worship God. But they also gather together to learn more about their religion, for group meetings, weddings, and funerals. The Star of David on the wall shows people that the synagogue is Jewish.'

Rees and Sara followed their friends through the synagogue doors.

The first thing Rees and Sara noticed was the clothes. All the men and boys were wearing a small circular cap called a kippah. Dan gave one to Rees to wear. All the men, older boys, and some women were wearing a prayer shawl called a tallit.

'We cover our heads to show that we are respectful and humble before God who is greater than anything else,' said Dan. 'The prayer shawl has four tassels which are tied with special knots. These tassels remind us of our duty to keep God's laws. These laws guide us through life. When I reach the age of thirteen I will wear a prayer shawl when I pray. Rebecca will wear one when she is twelve, if she wants to,' said Dan.

Dan and Rebecca took Rees and Sara to sit with the rest of their family.

The second thing that Rees and Sara noticed was an important-looking cabinet at the very front of the room. It looked important because its entrance was protected by a pair of gleaming gate-like doors. Behind the doors, Rees and Sara could see a finely-decorated, blue velvet curtain. Embroidered on the curtain were two regal lions, guarding two stone tablets. Sitting above the tablets was a crown.

'The cabinet is called the ark. Keep an eye on it. There is something very special inside,' said Rebecca. 'Can you see the ner tamid lamp burning above the ark? It is always kept alight. Its light is a symbol of God's presence here with us.'

Before long, everyone stood up and fixed their eyes on the ark. Some members of the congregation opened the ark's doors and drew back its curtain. There, standing in splendour, were enormous scrolls, covered in beautiful velvet mantles, breast plates, and finials.

'Those are our Torah scrolls. Each scroll contains the first five books of the Hebrew Bible,' said Rebecca in a hushed voice as one of the scrolls was carefully taken out. The scroll's mantle cover had a large tree embroidered on it. Its bells jingled as it moved.

'The Torah is often called the tree of life because its teachings offer a guide to life,' explained Dan. 'We believe that the Torah's teachings are very special because they are inspired by God.'

The Torah scroll was lifted up and carried in a procession to the reading desk. A member of the congregation acted as reader. Chanting carefully, he read a passage from the Torah in Hebrew. He followed the words with a silver pointer to avoid touching them with his fingers.

After the reading, the rabbi preached a sermon about it, and then there were prayers.

'The rabbi is a Jewish teacher and an expert in Jewish law,' explained Rebecca. 'The Torah is very old and the rabbi helps us to understand it by explaining what it means.'

At the synagogue Rees and Sara had learnt that Dan and Rebecca worship one God who is always with them. The Torah is their guide to life because it is inspired by God, and the rabbi is there to help them understand its teachings.

2 Celebrating Sukkot

Rees and Sara loved to make things. They could turn a cardboard box into an impressive mansion or an imposing castle. Pieces of paper could become a space shuttle carrying tourists to Mars or a fighter plane on a secret mission. They had almost made a tree house once. But their mother had stopped them because she said that it was 'definitely dangerous'.

It was early autumn and Rees and Sara were making something particularly exciting in Dan and Rebecca's back-garden. They were helping to build a special hut called a sukkah. Dan and Rebecca's family were getting ready to celebrate the Jewish festival of Sukkot and the hut would play an important part in the celebrations.

With the help of Dan and Rebecca's father and a picture, the children were putting the finishing touches to their hut. They laid leafy branches across the top to create a roof. A table and chairs were placed inside and an assortment of fruit and vegetables was hung from the ceiling. At last it was finished!

'In the Torah God asks us to celebrate the festival of Sukkot by living in simple huts for seven days,' said Dan. 'In Britain it is too cold and wet for us to spend all our time in the hut. So, many Jews obey God by spending some time each day in the hut, eating or relaxing with family and friends.'

Rees and Sara listened as Dan and Rebecca's father recited blessings over a cup of wine.

'This is the blessing for dwelling in the sukkah,' he said.

'Blessed are you, Lord, our God, king of the universe,
who has sanctified us with His commandments
and commanded us to dwell in the sukkah. Amen.'

'And this is another blessing which is said on the first night of the festival,' he added.

'Blessed are you, Lord, our God, king of the universe,
who has kept us alive, sustained us,
and enabled us to reach this season. Amen.'

After the blessings Rees and Sara were invited to share a meal with Dan and Rebecca's family in the sukkah.

As they sat around the small table eating supper, Rees and Sara learned more about the festival of Sukkot.

'Why does God ask you to live in a hut for seven days?' asked Rees, puzzled.

'Many, many years ago, our ancestors journeyed for 40 years in the wilderness. They travelled from Egypt to a land promised to them by God,' explained Dan. 'For 40 years our people lived in makeshift huts, which could be carried with them as they travelled. Our people experienced many hardships in the wilderness but God looked after them. When they were hungry, God provided quails and manna. When they were thirsty, God provided water.'

Rees and Sara looked upwards, through the leafy branches of the hut, and saw the stars. They imagined Dan and Rebecca's ancestors doing the same thing a long time ago.

'When we spend time in the sukkah, we remember the story of our people in the wilderness,' said Rebecca. 'We remember that just as God looked after them, God also looks after us. It is easy to forget this in our comfortable houses where we have enough to eat and enough to drink.'

Dan and Rebecca's mother gave Rees and Sara a second helping of food, and said, 'When we spend time in the sukkah, we remember that our people were God's guests in the wilderness. God gave them food to eat and water to drink. We remember this by inviting guests to our sukkah and offering them something to eat and something to drink. Tonight, Rees and Sara are our guests.'

Dan performed the Blessing of the Four Species.

'Blessed are you, Lord, our God, king of the universe,
who has sanctified us with His commandments
and commanded us to take up the lulav. Amen.'

In one hand Dan held the branches of three plants – palm,
myrtle, and willow. In his other hand he held a fruit called an etrog.
These were waved in six directions – north, south, east, west, up,
and down.

'Dan is rejoicing before God,' explained Rebecca. 'The plants are
waved in all directions to show that God is everywhere.'

Rees and Sara enjoyed building the sukkah and eating in it. They
learnt that Sukkot celebrates the way God looked after Dan and
Rebecca's ancestors in the wilderness. But the most important
thing is that Dan and Rebecca believe that God still looks after
them today.

3 Understanding the Torah

For a brother and sister, Rees and Sara got on quite well. But today was different. They had spent most of the morning arguing about important little things.

8am   Sara insists on keeping the toy from the cereal box. Rees and Sara argue.

8.30am   Rees kicks a football into Sara's face by accident. Sara and Rees argue.

9.30am   Sara refuses to move so that Rees can see the television. Rees and Sara argue.

10.45am   Sara discovers her junior microscope under Rees's bed. Rees and Sara argue.

11.00am   Rees and Sara's mother says that she is fed up with both of them. Everyone argues.

11.15am   Rees, Sara, and their mother agree on three rules to stop arguments, and they pin these rules up on the wall. They all promise to try to keep these rules.

Later, Rees and Sara went round to Dan and Rebecca's house. Dan and Rebecca listened with interest as Rees and Sara told them about their new family rules. Rebecca was thoughtful.

'As Jews, Dan and I have rules we try to follow too,' she said. 'We called them commandments. These commandments have been given to us by God, and they help us to live fairly and peacefully with others. The commandments are found in our sacred book, the Torah.'

Rebecca told Rees and Sara that there are 613 commandments in the Torah.

'The most famous commandments in the Torah are called the Ten Commandments,' she said. 'Jews believe that they were given to Moses by God on Mount Sinai. The first four commandments deal with our relationship with God.'

Rebecca listed them.

1   I am the LORD your God. You shall have no other gods besides me.
2   You shall not make false gods or worship them.
3   You shall not make wrongful use of the name of the LORD your God.
4   Keep the Sabbath day holy.

'We need these commandments to remind us to worship only one God, who is creator and Lord of all,' she explained. 'If we keep these four commandments, we are more likely to keep the other commandments, because we remember that they come from God.'

'Yes,' agreed Dan. 'God always knows what is best for us. The last six commandments are all about our relationship with other people.' Dan listed them.

5   Honour your father and mother.
6   You shall not murder.
7   You shall not commit adultery.
8   You shall not steal.
9   You shall not bear false witness against your neighbour.
10 You shall not covet anything that belongs to your neighbour.

'Our people have promised to keep God's commandments. We know that when we keep God's commandments we set a good example to others and bring honour to God. It is a big responsibility!' said Dan.

Rees and Sara thought about their new family rules and Dan and Rebecca's commandments. They could see two serious problems with rules and commandments. The first serious problem is that they can be difficult to understand properly. How do you keep the Sabbath day holy? How do you honour your father and mother?

Sara asked Dan and Rebecca, 'So, who helps you to understand the 613 commandments? Who explains what they mean?'

'We have rabbis who are Jewish teachers and experts in the law,' answered Dan. 'Rabbis have helped us to understand God's commandments for centuries and they continue to help us understand God's commandments today.'

The second serious problem is that rules and commandments are easily broken.

'What happens if you break God's commandments?' asked Rees.

'When we break God's commandments, in the Torah God asks us to repent,' answered Rebecca. 'This means that we feel sorry for what we have done. After this, we decide that we will not do it again. Then, we try to repair the damage we have done to whoever we have wronged. Hopefully, after this, whoever we have wronged will forgive us.'

Rees and Sara had learnt some new things about Dan and Rebecca. They had learnt that 613 commandments are found in the Torah. These commandments remind Jews to worship one God and they help them to get on with other people. Many Jews have promised to keep these commandments. If they break a commandment, they need to repent and be forgiven by whoever they have wronged.

4 Caring for others and the world

Rees and Sara were standing outside Dan and Rebecca's front door. As they waited for their friends to answer the door bell, Rees spotted something that he had not seen before.

'What is that?' asked Rees, pointing at a metal plaque nailed to the right hand side of the door.

Sara inspected it closely and shrugged her shoulders.

'I have no idea,' she said.

At that moment the front door swung open, revealing Dan and Rebecca.

'You are looking at our mezuzah!' exclaimed Rebecca. 'Jewish buildings and homes should have a mezuzah on the door post. Inside each mezuzah there is a scroll which has some important verses from the Torah written on it. These verses are called the Shema which begins like this.

> 'Hear, O Israel, the Lord is our God, the Lord is one.
> And you shall love the Lord your God
> with all your heart, with all your soul, and with all your might.'

Rees and Sara were puzzled.

'Why do you nail those words to your door posts?' asked Rees.

'God asks us to do this in the Torah for an important reason,' said Rebecca. 'The mezuzah is there to remind us to obey God's commandments.'

Dan and Rebecca took Rees and Sara to the dining room.

'We are having a family meeting,' said Dan.

They joined Dan and Rebecca's parents who were seated at the table. On the table there were leaflets advertising the work of various charities. Some charities help children. Other charities help animals. Some charities research into dangerous illnesses and diseases. Other charities support communities in faraway places. Dan and Rebecca's family were trying to choose two charities to support.

In the very centre of the table was a box.

'That is our charity box,' explained Dan. 'We put money into it whenever we can. We love and serve God by the way we act. One way we love and serve God is by looking after the things that God has created. This means looking after people, animals, and the environment.'

Dan and Rebecca's father spoke and everyone listened.

'In the Torah God has given us many commandments about how we should treat other people,' he said. 'The most important commandment is this – You shall love your neighbour as yourself. This means more than just not harming people. We are also expected to help people as often as we can. Charity is an important part of Jewish law.'

After a discussion, Dan and Rebecca and their parents agreed to give some of their money to a charity working with children.

Then, Dan and Rebecca's mother spoke and everyone listened.

'In the Torah God has given us many commandments about treating animals and the environment with respect and care,' she said. 'But one of my favourite Jewish teachings does not come from the Torah. It contains an important message for all of us today.'

Dan and Rebecca's mother read aloud this passage from Ecclesiastes Rabbah:

'Look at My creations! See how beautiful and perfect they are!
For your sake I created them all.
Do not desolate and corrupt My world,
for if you corrupt it there is no one to set it right after you.'

Everyone thought about the wonderful world in which they lived. They thought about oceans, forests, and skies, all teeming with life.

Dan and Rebecca's mother continued.

'The world provides us with everything we need,' she said. 'But we need to look after the world carefully. The world is easily destroyed if we take too much from it or if we pollute it. The world is our responsibility!'

After a discussion, Dan and Rebecca and their parents agreed to give some of their money to a charity concerned with preserving rain forests. They also agreed that the family would make a bigger effort to recycle as many things as possible.

The family meeting had given Rees and Sara a lot to think about. Dan and Rebecca love and serve God by obeying God's commandments. They are commanded in the Torah to look after God's creation which includes people, animals, and the environment. One way they look after God's creation is by giving money to charity as often as possible.

24

5 Learning about kashrut

Rees and Sara were feeling very happy. Their Aunty Hafwen had come to stay for a few days and she had promised to take them somewhere special.

After a long discussion, Rees and Sara agreed to travel a few miles outside the town to a small farm which was open to visitors. Apparently, there were lots of exciting things to do there.

'Please may our friends, Dan and Rebecca, come too?' begged Sara.

'Of course they can,' agreed Aunty Hafwen, smiling.

Later that day, Rees and Sara learned all sorts of new skills with Dan and Rebecca. They were taught how to milk cows. They carefully groomed some horses and were even allowed a short ride. They fed some tiny lambs with bottles of milk and watched sheep being sheared.

After this, everyone felt tired and hungry. So, Aunty Hafwen suggested a snack and a drink in the farm café.

Sitting in the farm café, they looked closely at the menu.

'Dan and I need to be careful about what we eat,' said Rebecca. 'This is because Jews have food laws called kashrut and these affect what we eat.'

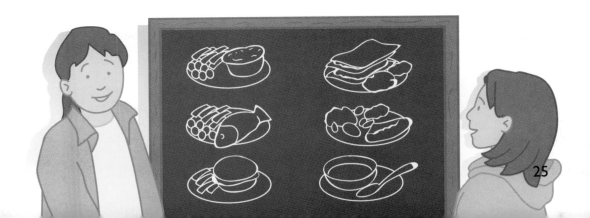

25

'Tell us more about your food laws,' said Aunty Hafwen. 'Then, we can all search the menu for something for you to eat.'

Dan thought carefully before he spoke. He knew that food laws are quite complicated.

'In our sacred book, the Torah, there are many food laws,' said Dan. 'These food laws can be divided into two main groups. The first group of laws deals with the kinds of food we are allowed to eat. For example, the Torah says that we are allowed to eat cows, goats, chickens, ducks, fish with fins and scales, deer, and sheep but we are not allowed to eat pigs. We can eat all fruit and vegetables though.'

Sara checked the menu.

'So you cannot eat any sausages or bacon, but there are lots of other things here that you can eat,' she said.

Dan laughed. 'It is not quite as simple as that,' he said. 'This is because of the second group of laws which deal with the way we prepare food. For example, the Torah says that we should eat only the meat of animals that have been killed and checked in a special Jewish way. Also, Jews should not eat meat and dairy products in the same meal.'

Rees checked the menu.

'It is probably a good idea to have something vegetarian,' he suggested.

Dan and Rebecca agreed and they chose vegetable casserole.

As they ate, Rebecca told Rees and Sara some more about Jewish food laws.

'Our family is not very strict about keeping all the Jewish food laws because we are Reform Jews,' she said. 'But we always try to make sure that we do not eat meat from pigs and that animals have been killed according to the Jewish way. We have an uncle who is a much stricter Orthodox Jew. You should see his kitchen!'

Rebecca described how Uncle Reuben took the mixing of meat and dairy products very seriously indeed. He even used different dishes and cooking utensils for different kinds of food. Dishes and cooking utensils used for meat were stored on one side of the kitchen. Dishes and cooking utensils used for dairy products were stored on the other side of the kitchen.

Rees wanted to know why Jews have food laws.

'Some people believe that the Jewish way of eating is healthy and that is why God has asked for it in the Torah. But this is not a very good argument,' said Dan. 'Our family keeps some of the food laws because they make us feel Jewish and God has asked us to.'

Rees and Sara enjoyed visiting the farm with Dan and Rebecca and Aunty Hafwen. They now understood their Jewish friends much better. They had learnt that many Jews keep food laws called kashrut and these are found in the Torah. But not all Jews are the same. Some Jews keep the food laws more strictly than others.

That evening, before Rees and Sara went to sleep, they agreed that they would start sharing some of their own special things with Dan and Rebecca. Maybe tomorrow...

In the World Faiths Today Series Rees and Sara learn about the major world faiths in their own country. The seven stories in the series are:

- Exploring Islam
- Exploring Judaism
- Exploring the Parish Church
- Exploring the Orthodox Church
- Exploring Hinduism
- Exploring Buddhism
- Exploring Sikhism

Welsh National Centre for Religious Education
Bangor University
Bangor
Gwynedd
Wales

First published 2008.

Sponsored by the Welsh Assembly Government.

British Library Cataloguing-in-Publication Data
A catalogue record for this book is available from the British Library.

ISBN 978-1-85357-180-0

Printed and bound in Wales by Gwasg Dwyfor.